I Love Me

Little King Lee!

Building Self-Esteem In Children

Written by: Latrice Slaughter

Illustrated by: Terry Did'Um

Printed and Bound in the United States of America

Published and Distrubuted By
Lioness Publishing
Email: livia.latrice@gmail.com

Packaging/Consulting
Lioness Publishing
livia.latrice@gmail.com

Cover Design: Terry Did'Um Bolen
irockjesus@att.net
First Printing Stepember 2016
978-0-9961606-1-2
10987654321

For inquires contact: livia.latrice@gmail.com

Dedications

Daddy, I'm grateful that I can say I have had a father in my life that gave me the love that only a father can give. Thank you for always being there. Love you always.

To my Grandfather Victor Rockett, I hear so many stories of your strength, your courage, your fearlessness, the respect you gained in your community from both whites and blacks during a time where blacks had to fight to gain equal rights. I have a fearless nature and I know a lot of that came from you.

Terry DidUm Bolen, this project would not have been a success without your beautiful gift. Thank you for being the vessel used by God to help me bring his message forth. I appreciate you.

Kalief Browder, I read your story and was heartbroken to know that you had suffered silently for so long. I also dedicate this book to you. You will always be a king. Rest easy with the creator, the ancestors, and the angels. You are loved.

It was placed on my heart to write this book for every little boy. Know this little ones, whatever obstacles life decides to give you, trust that it will build your character and make you strong.
On your worst days, the days that you feel like giving up, the days when you feel like no one cares, the days when you are all alone remember, YOU ARE A KING!

Hi there! My name is little King Lee! I'm a little King and I love me!

I love me...
I love me...
I love me...me...me...

I will tell you why
I love me the way
that I do.

From the top of my head to the bottom of my shoes.

I have ten fingers
and ten toes.

Thick Curly Hair,

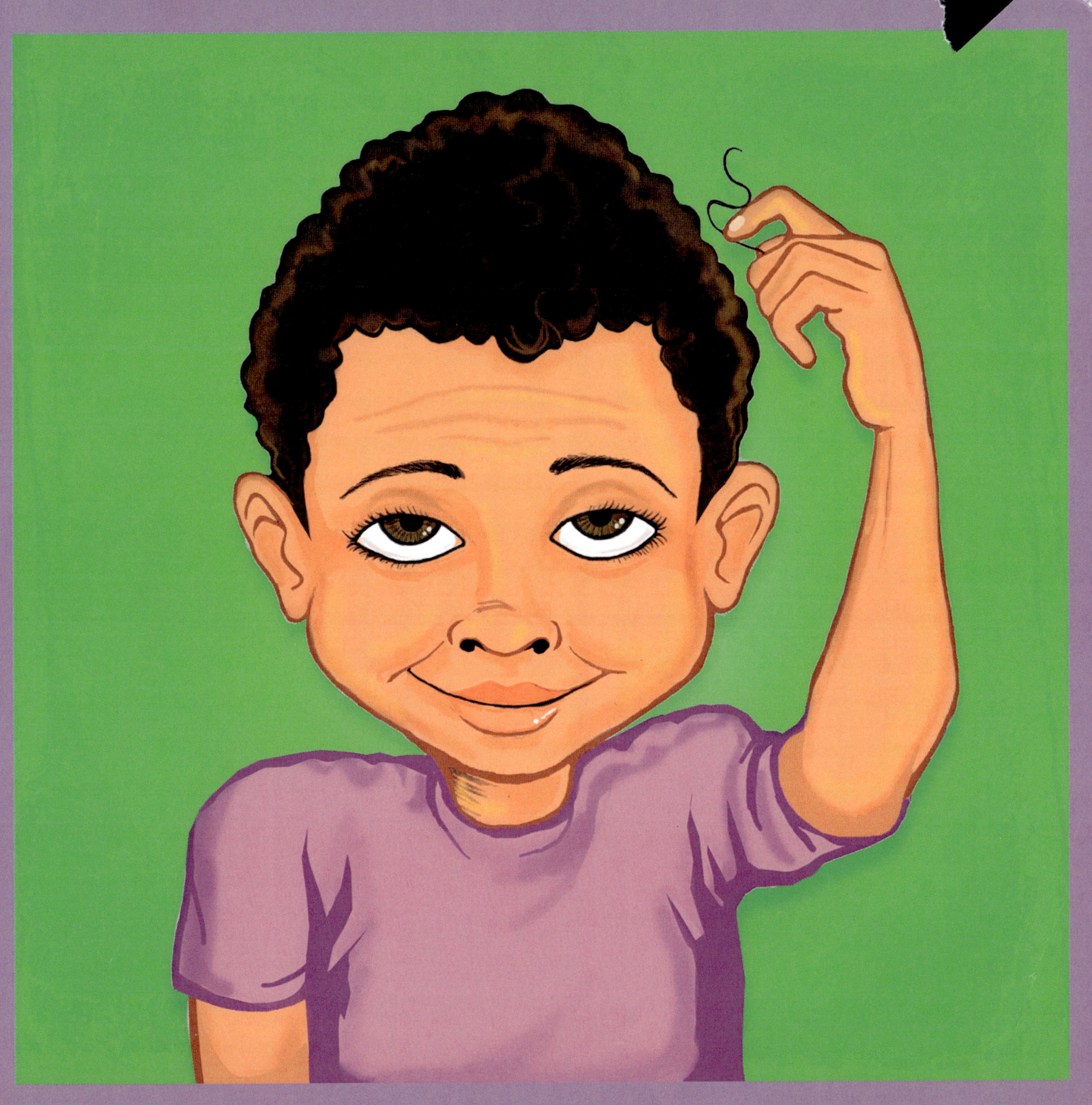

And a cute little nose.

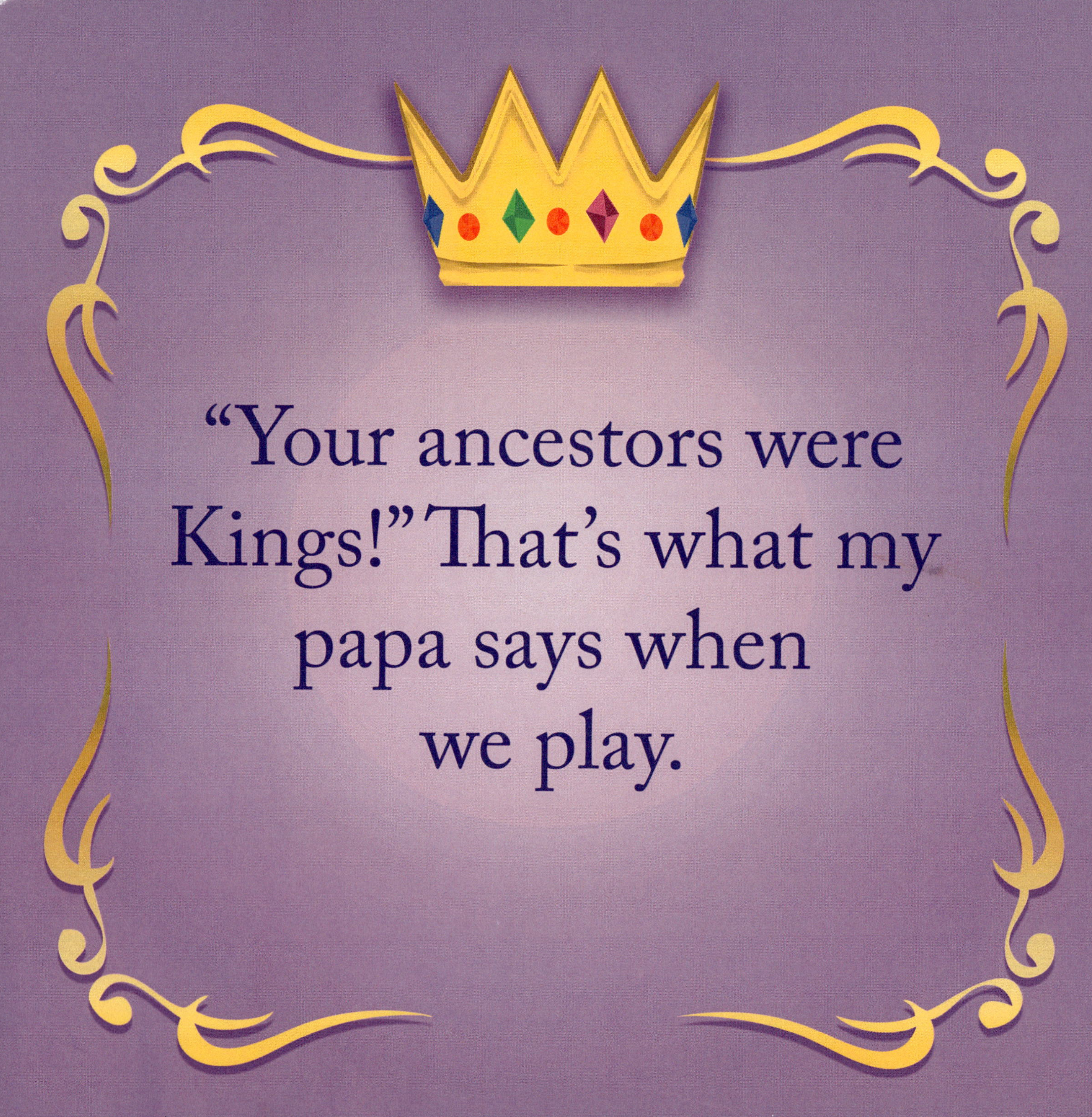

“Your ancestors were Kings!” That’s what my papa says when we play.

So I order my little brothers to beat the royal drums as I dance the night away.

Or at least until bedtime.

I love my eyes
and I love my hair.
I love my color
and that's why I stare

in the mirror sometimes
because I am pleased,
you see?

I would never want to
be anyone else because
I love me!

You should love you too! After all, there is only one you!

From the top of your head to the bottom of your shoes.

So the next time you're feeling sad and not being the very best you can be,

Just look in the mirror
and say "I love me!"

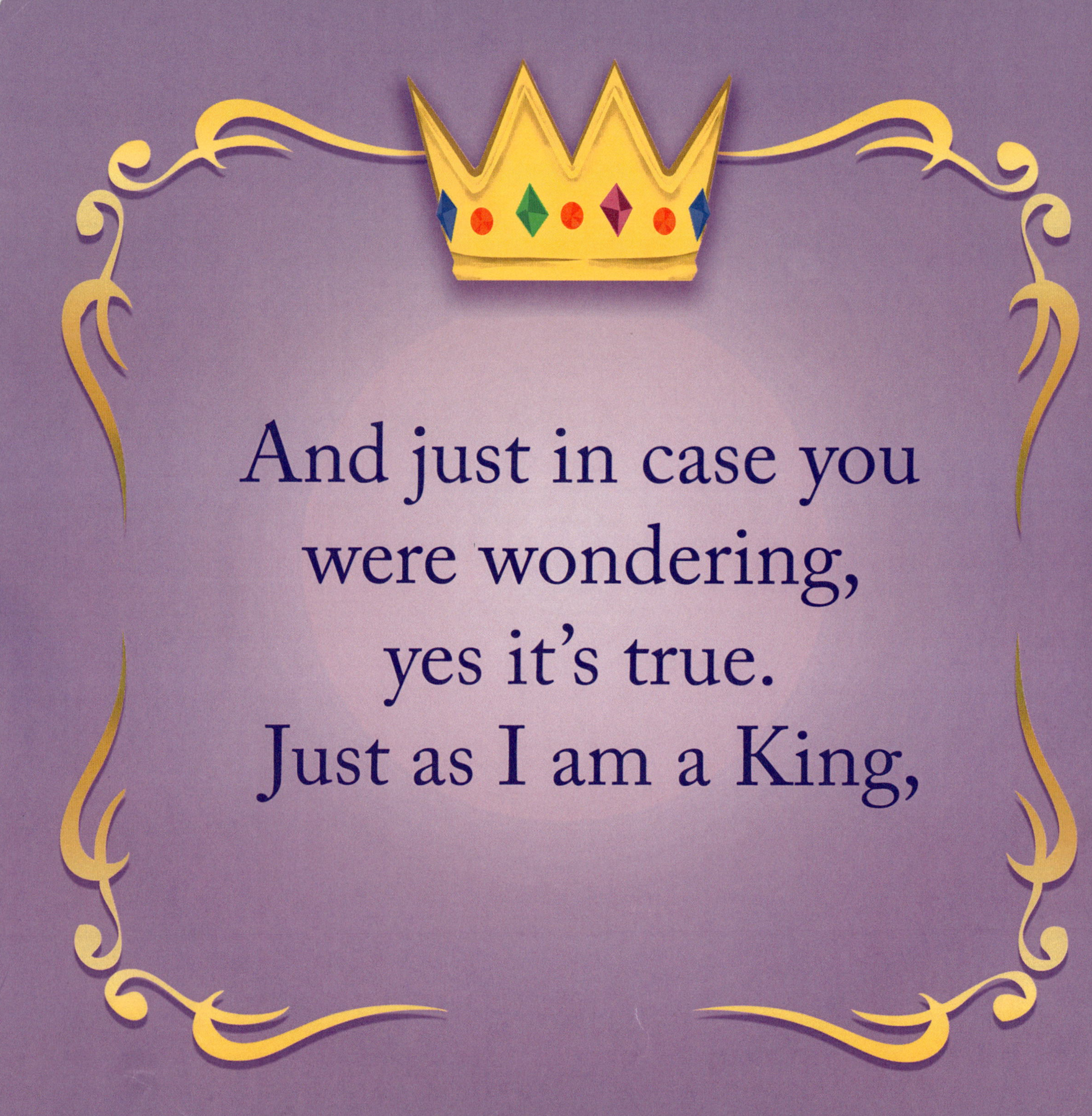

And just in case you
were wondering,
yes it's true.
Just as I am a King,

Your picture

So are you!

Made in the USA
Coppell, TX
21 December 2020